Of Mice and Rats

By Allan Fowler

Consultants

Linda Cornwell, Learning Resource Consultant,
Indiana Department of Education

Janann V. Jenner, Ph.D.

Sharyn Fenwick, Elementary Science/Math Specialist
Gustavus Adolphus College, St. Peter, Minnesota

Children's Press®
A Division of Grolier Publishing
New York   London   Hong Kong   Sydney
Danbury, Connecticut

Visit Children's Press® on the Internet at:
http://publishing.grolier.com

Designer: Herman Adler Design Group
Photo Researcher: Caroline Anderson

Library of Congress Cataloging-in-Publication Data

Fowler, Allan.
    Of mice and rats / by Allan Fowler.
        p. cm. — (Rookie read-about science)
    Includes index.
    Summary: Contrasts the characteristics of a wide variety of mice and rats.
    ISBN 0-516-20800-4 (lib. bdg.)   0-516-26418-4 (pbk.)
    1. Mice—Juvenile literature. 2. Rats—Juvenile literature.
  [1. Rats.] I. Title. II. Series.
  QL737.R6F68   1998   97-28658
  599.35—dc21   .   CIP
                                         AC

Almost everybody likes Mickey Mouse. He's cute, he's friendly, and he makes us laugh. But real mice are often a different story.

Some people like mice so
much they keep them as pets.

But when mice show up in a home uninvited, they are usually thought of as pests.

Mice are so small that they
can fit almost anywhere.
They use their sense of
smell to find food.

They will nibble away at even the tiniest crumbs.

They can also damage clothing, books, and other things by gnawing on them.

Some mice carry diseases that can make people sick.

As you can easily guess from its name, the house mouse prefers to live indoors. It has grayish or brownish hair, but its thin tail looks hairless.

The tail of a house mouse is about the same length as its body. A good-sized house mouse, along with its tail, would reach from one side of this page to the other.

The harvest mouse is a bit smaller than the house mouse. It lives in grassy fields.

Another country mouse is
the vole, or field mouse.

Female mice give birth as often as eight times a year. Each litter consists of 3 to 11 young mice.

That means a single mouse could have 88 babies in a single year!

Rats look a lot like mice,
but rats are much larger.

Most people don't
like rats because they
spread diseases.

People can get these
diseases if a rat bites them.

They can also get sick
if they are bitten by one
of the tiny fleas that live
on a rat's body.

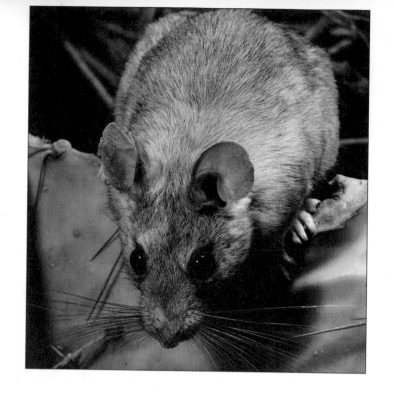

Rats can live just about
anywhere. Some live
in fields and forests.
Others live on farms.

Farmers do their best
to keep rats away. They
don't want rats to eat their
chickens' eggs or the grain
they have in storage.

Many rats live in large cities. They can be found in buildings or in places where garbage is dumped.

Others stay underground,
in sewers or tunncls.

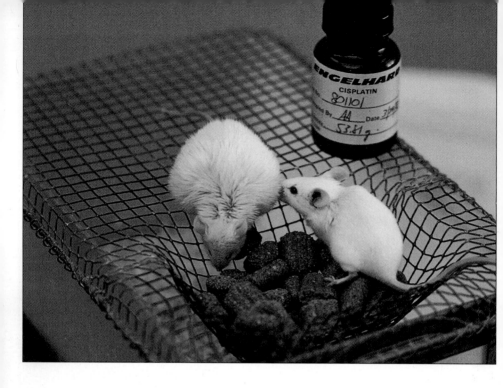

Rats are also found in
medical laboratories.
Scientists often test new
medicines on them.

Water rats live in small holes, which they dig along riverbanks.

The most common type
of rat is the brown rat.

Brown rats—also called
Norway rats—are not always
brown. They may also be
black, gray, or white. Some
brown rats are 10 inches
long, not counting the tail.

Black rats aren't as common as brown rats. They are smaller and more gentle, so brown rats often drive them away.

Rats are very strong for their size. They are excellent climbers and can leap quite far. They can even swim.

Like mice, rats often
have lots of babies.

City health departments
have a hard time keeping
the rat population down.
In North America, there
are more rats than people.

Rats and mice belong to a group of animals called rodents.

All rodents have four large front teeth—two upper and two lower—to gnaw with.

Gnawing wears down the front teeth . . .

. . . but that's no problem.
A rodent's teeth never
stop growing.

Words You Know

laboratory

litter

rodent

sewer

harvest mouse

house mouse

black rat

brown rat

water rat

vole

Index

About the Author

Allan Fowler is a freelance writer with a background in advertising.
Born in New York, he lives in Chicago now and enjoys traveling.

Photo Credits

©: Animals Animals: 4 (Henry Ausloos), 16 (Paul & Shirley Berquist),
23 (Breck P. Kent), 11, 31 bottom right (Robert Maier), 14 (Robin Redfern);
BBC Natural History Unit: 27 (John Downer), 18, 19, 30 bottom right
(Warwick Sloss); Ellis Nature Photography: 5, 6, 12, 13, 30 top right
(Michael Durham); National Geographic: 20, 30 top left (James L. Amos);
Photo Researchers: 8, 17, 25, 26, 31 top right (Stephen Dalton), 9, 22, 24, 29,
30 bottom left, 31 center left, 31 center right, (Tom McHugh), 10, 31 top left
(Anthony Merceca); Photofest: 3; Tony Stone Images: cover (Rod Planck),
21, 31 bottom left (Gay Bumgarner).